"Tiger Woods has exploded onto the professional golf scene with the impact of a nuclear bomb. His game is huge and the record books will change with every step he takes. Ben Hogan, Arnold Palmer, Sam Snead, Jack Nicklaus, Gary Player, Lee Trevino, Tom Watson, and Greg Norman carried golf to new levels in their own right. But...move over boys, Tiger takes this game into the new millennium and beyond. Bet on it!" *Eddie Merrins, PGA Professional, Bel Air Country Club, Los Angeles, California*

TIGER

Reflections on a Champion

Edited by David LaFontaine

DOVE
B O O K S

TABLE OF CONTENTS

VITAL STATISTICS

Eldrick "Tiger" Woods
Birthplace: Cypress, California
Residence: Orlando, Florida
Born: December 30, 1975
High School: Western High School
College: Stanford University
Height: 6'2"
Weight: 150 pounds
Father's Name: Earl
Mother's: Kultida

AGES 2-5

- Appeared on *CBS Network News* and *The Mike Douglas Show* putting with Bob Hope (age 2)
- Shot score of 48 for 9 holes on U.S. Navy golf course (age 3)
- Appeared on TV's *That's Incredible* (age 5)

AGES 6-13

- Appeared on the *Today* show, *Good Morning America,* ESPN, CBS, NBC, ABC
- Won Optimist Junior World at ages 8, 9, 12, and 13
- Finished 2nd - Insurance Youth Golf Classic (Big "I") National at 13

AGE 14

- 1st place: Optimist International Junior World (5th time)
- 1st place: Insurance Youth Golf Classic (Big "I") National (record youngest ever to win)
- 2nd place: PGA National Junior Championship
- Semifinalist at USGA Junior National Championship
- Southern California Player of the Year

AGE 15

- 1st place: U.S. Junior National Championship (youngest ever to win)
- 1st place: Optimist Junior World (6th time)
- 1st place: CIF-SCGA High School Invitational Championship (Individual)
- 1st place: Southern California Championship
- 1st place: Ping/Phoenix Junior (AJGA)
- 1st place: Edgewood Tahoe Junior Classic (AJGA)

- 1st place: Los Angeles City Junior Championship
- 1st place: Orange Bowl Junior International
- AJGA Player of the Year
- Golf Digest Player of the Year
- Southern California Player of the Year
- Titleist–GolfWeek National Amateur of the Year
- 1st Team: Rolex Junior All-American

AGE 16

- 1st place: USGA Junior National Championship
- 1st place: Southern California Junior Best Ball Championship
- 1st place: Nabisco Mission Hills Desert Junior (AJGA)
- 1st place: Pro Gear San Antonio Shootout (AJGA)
- 1st place: Insurance Youth Golf Classic (Big "I") National
- 2nd place: Optimist Junior International World
- 5th place: Sunnehanna Amateur Tournament of Champions
- Top 32: 1992 U.S. Amateur
- AJGA Player of the Year
- Golf Digest Player of the Year

- Southern California Player of the Year
- Titleist–GolfWeek National Amateur of the Year
- GolfWorld Player of the Year

AGE 17

- 1st place: USGA Junior National Championship
- 1st place: Southern California Junior Best Ball Championship
- 2nd place: AJGA Taylor Made Woodlands
- Top 32: 1993 U.S. Amateur
- 1st Team: Rolex Junior All-American (4th consecutive year)
- Southern California Player of the Year
- GolfWorld Player of the Year
- Winner, Dial Award

AGE 18

- 1st place: U.S. Amateur
- 1st place: Western Amateur Championship
- 1st place: Southern California Golf Championship
- 1st place: Pacific Northwest Amateur Championship
- 1st place: CIF Southern Section Championship

- Semifinalist: California State Amateur Championship
- 16th place: Porter Cup
- Los Angeles Times Player of the Year
- Orange County Player of the Year
- Orange County League Most Valuable Player
- 1st place: William Tucker Invitational at Albuquerque
- Member, U.S. Team at the World Amateur Championships in Versailles, France
- GolfWorld Man of the Year

AGE 19

- 1st place: U.S. Amateur
- Golf's Amateur Representative for the Sullivan Award
- tied for 41st place in the Masters in Augusta, 1995
- tied for 5th place at the NCAA Championships in Columbus, Ohio
- tied for 67th place at the British Open at St. Andrews
- Pac-10 Player of the Year
- First Team All-American
- Stanford's 1995 Male Freshman of the Year (all sports)
- Preseason First Team All-American for 95–96 by *GolfWeek Magazine*

AGE 20

- 1st place: U.S. Amateur
- Became professional August 28, 1996
- 60th place: Milwaukee Open
- 11th place: Canadian Open
- 5th place: Quad City Classic
- 3rd place: BC Open
- 1st place: Las Vegas Invitational
- 3rd place: La Cantera Texas Open
- 1st place: Walt Disney Oldsmobile Classic
- 21st place: Tour Championship
- PGA Rookie of the Year

AGE 21

- 1st place: Mercedes Championship
- tied for 18th place: Phoenix Open
- tied for 2nd place: Pebble Beach National Pro-Am
- tied for 20th: Nissan Open
- tied for 9th: Bay Hill Invitational
- tied for 31st place: Players Championship
- 1st place: The Masters

INTRODUCTION

Tiger Woods.

Like any phenomenon, he's being chewed over and digested and analyzed from so many angles in our information-overload society. He is being made to stand for so much, subject to being built up and torn down in the same story (sometimes in the same sentence), so it's easy to lose the perspective on just what the story is. The story, in retrospect, all seems like such a clear inevitable progression. From infant prodigy to child phenomenon to college champion to adult superstar. It all seems so straight and focused—like Tiger himself—so ordained, even, that we sometimes lose sight of the fact that for all the trophies and championships and stories and ad campaigns, Tiger Woods is a young man. And like every young man, he's making it all up as he goes along.

Tiger wouldn't like that last bit, of course; he prefers to think of himself not as making it up, but making it happen. Visualizing his outcome and acting on his dreams. But that's something you'll learn by reading this book. It's about what Tiger does and how he does it, by Tiger himself, and by the people who best know him and his game of golf.

I. TIGER CUB

RICK REILLY, EDITOR:

"The 'Tiger' was given to him by his father in honor of his father's Vietnam combat partner, Nguyen Phong of the South Vietnamese Army. Earl nicknamed Phong 'Tiger' for his unblinking bravery.

"It was Tiger who took him on an insane mission through the streets of a VC-held village and got himself the Silver Star. It was Tiger, his best friend, who pulled him off a rice-paddy dike seconds after sniper fire tore over him.

"Around 1967 or '68, they lost contact, but Earl is convinced Tiger is still alive somewhere in the world. And so he nicknamed his own son Tiger in hopes that someday Nguyen Phong would pick up a newspaper and read about Earl's famous son, the greatest golfer who ever lived, and understand. . . ."

—Sports Illustrated, *March 27, 1995*

KULTIDA:

"Every mother thinks their child is special, no matter what they do. Tiger first swung a golf club when he was only 6 months old."

—Time *magazine's international edition, April 14, 1997*

TIM CROTHERS:

"Legend has it that at age two, Tiger shot a 48 on the back nine of the navy golf course, in his hometown of Cypress, CA. When his father senses an audit coming, he admits that his son played from the red tees and that every shot in the fairway was teed up. Uh-huh."

—People, *March 25, 1991*

EARL WOODS:

"It was uncanny that way he could emulate my swing. It was like looking at myself in a miniature mirror."

—People, *March 25, 1991*

"There is evidence, scientific and anecdotal, that, in order to succeed at golf, or any other game involving skill, you cannot start early enough. The sports scientists say that, while the development of ability varies from sport to sport and child to child, there are two vital stages. First come the 'motor-skill acquisition years,' which last from birth until four. Later come the 'heart–lung muscle development years,' which begin at puberty.

"Many believe that all the skills that one will ever have are acquired by the age of four. And new skills developed after that age, from playing a game to flying a plane, are just new combinations of skills already learnt."

—London Times, *May 1, 1997*

KEVIN COSTNER IN TIN CUP:

"The first thing you gotta learn about this game is that it ain't about hitting some little white ball in some yonder hole. It's about inner demons, self-doubt, human frailty, and overcoming all that crap."

L.A. SPORTSCASTER JIM HILL, WHEN TIGER WAS AGE 3:

"This young man is going to be to golf what Jimmy Connors and Chris Evert are to tennis."

—*KCBS Archives*

"After the Jim Hill report, Tiger appeared on *The Mike Douglas Show,* and stole the show from Bob Hope in a putting contest. At five, *That's Incredible* did a segment on him.

"He also appeared on the *Today* show, *Good Morning America,* ESPN, CBS, NBC, and ABC—all before he was 13. He won the Optimist International Junior World when he was 8, 9, 12, and 13."

—Nike press release, July 1996

"When Woods was 11, Earl put him through a six-month boot camp to instill mental toughness.

'Prisoner-of-war interrogation techniques, psychological intimidation—it went on and on. It was brutal,' Earl says."

—People, April 28, 1997

"His father, Earl, a former Green Beret, put his son through a series of mental drills many years ago, tests that if not for Tiger's eager participation, would have seemed abusive. But when the training ended, Earl assured his son, 'Nobody will ever be mentally tougher than you are.' "

—Titleist publicity release on Tiger, November 1996

"When the boy was six, he asked his parents for the subliminal tape. In the parent's plan to raise the greatest golfer who ever lived, the boy's mind had to be trained.

"When the boy was seven, his parents installed the psychological armor. If he had a full wedge shot, the father would stand 15 feet in front of him and say 'I'm a tree.' And the kid would have to hit over him. The father would jingle his change before the boy's bunker shots. Pump the brake on the cart on the boy's mid-irons. Rip the Velcro on his glove over a three-footer.

"What his dad tried to do, whenever possible, was cheat, distract, harass, and annoy him.

"What the father wanted for his son was the one thing he had had in battle, the thing that had kept Charlie from putting him in a bag: a 'dark side,' as he calls it, 'a coldness.' "

—Sports Illustrated, *March 27, 1995*

TIGER:

"I'm like my dad in that we both get icy under pressure. I don't want to sound cocky, but that's what I love the most, doing it when it means the most."

—*Associated Press, February 20, 1997*

SPORTS PSYCHOLOGIST JAY BRUNZA:

"Tiger shouldn't be portrayed as the Robo-Golfer. He doesn't need motivation from anybody else; his is internal. I don't see him burning out, because golf is pure pleasure for him."

—People, *March 25, 1991*

"He had a middle-class upbringing by his real parents, Jor-El and Lara, on the planet Krypton."

—Entertainment Weekly, *April 28, 1997*

"Buddhism has given me the inner peace and calmness I probably wouldn't have achieved at such an early age, and I owe that to my mom."

—Sports Illustrated Online Plus, *February 17, 1997*

Rudy Duran, Tiger's childhood coach:

"I saw a kid who popped out of the womb a Magic Johnson or a Wolfgang Amadeus Mozart. He had talent oozing out of his fingertips."

—People, *April 28, 1997*

Butch Harmon, Tiger's swing coach:

"Tiger was born with a beautiful natural flow to his swing. It enables him to come through the ball almost like the crack of a whip. Add to that the fact that he was taught well early, because Earl had a real good concept of the golf swing."

—People, *April 28, 1997*

"I just love to compete. I don't care if it's golf or Nintendo or in the classroom. I mean, competing against the other students or competing against myself. I know what I'm capable of.

"You know, the prize money, that's the paycheck. That's the money I earned for myself. All the other stuff, my Nike contract and Titleist and now the All Star Cafe, to me, that's a bank account, but it doesn't really make me as happy as what I earn through blood, sweat, and tears on the golf course. That money, I have the sole responsibility for earning that. Just me, alone. All the other stuff can depend on how good your agent is."

—Business Week

Earl Woods:

"I'll be satisfied if he's just a great person. I don't give a shit about golf. I'm not worried now. Obviously, I will not be here to see the final result. I will see enough to know that I've done a good job."

—GQ

Paul Goydos:

"Tiger is like John Daly but with total control. If that's not a scary prospect for the rest of us, I don't know what is."

—Golf Digest, *April 1997*

TIGER ON MATCH PLAY:

"It's just a matter of timing. You have to have the ability in match play to read what your opponent is doing and adjust . . . basically, you can play it two ways. One, you can struggle with it and beat your brains out. Or two, you can adapt. Match play is not 18 holes, it is 18-hole matches. You have to approach it that way. Each hole is a match."

"That's what match play is. You can get killed or you can kill someone. Or it can be anywhere in between. That's what makes match play so much fun."

"I am always nervous on the first tee shot. After that, I am fine . . . people asked me if I would be intimidated or overwhelmed playing with these people. And I said 'No.' One reason is the fact that the game does not change—low score wins. And that's the way I am going to go out and approach it. That's the way I have always approached it and I am not going to change."

—Press Conference via Golf.com, the Internet page of USGA, April 21, 1995

II. TURNING PRO

"It all set in last week when they announced me on the tee not as an amateur. I knew it was a job now. I had a tough two weeks. I got my first rest here, this week. All the other players have met me with open arms. All the guys I know here are always nice and positive. It was hard leaving school, and my friends. Plus, there are not frat parties on tour."

—*Bell Canadian Open Press Conference via the Internet*

"It is that focus, that attitude that ensures that Tiger Woods has only just started to win major championships. Virtually no player can outhit him and virtually no player can outthink him. And he cares about only one thing: winning."

—Newsday, *April 15, 1997*

TIGER ON TAKING ON GOLF AS A CAREER:

"When you have kids come up to you and say 'I'm playing golf because of you,' you know you've made a difference. It's nice to be able to touch people that way. You can always learn something about this game. I'm not a person who likes to say no to people. But I also have to be careful. I'm out here to work and accomplish something."

—*Bell Canadian Open Press Conference via the Internet*

TOM WATSON WHEN TIGER WAS IN COLLEGE:

"Tiger's heard some stories about me at Stanford. Like, 'Is is true on the 9th hole you hit the 12th fairway?'

"I could hit it long and I could putt, but I didn't have a clue. When I came out on tour in 1971, I didn't know how to win. I wanted to make the top 60. My sponsors put up 18 grand, and I wanted to pay it back and make some money."

"Money is a corrupter. It certainly complicates things. I know if we (including Fred Couples and John Daly) didn't have any money, the three of us would be better players. I don't know about Tiger."

—Stanford University press release

TIGER ON TURNING PRO:

"Going into the Amateur, I knew that I would make a decision after the Amateur—should I or shouldn't I? I knew that after I won, there was not much to achieve in amateur golf.

"A difficult part arose out of the need to deal with the question, Should I become a professional golfer? It helped me grow and think about all aspects of the decision.

"I'm leaving some of my best friends. I can't hop over to their place at 11 at night and hang out with them. That I will miss.

"I do have goals. Obviously one is to try to make the tour. Anything more specific I can't share with you because they're personal."

—GolfWeb via the Internet

NIKE CHAIRMAN PHIL KNIGHT:

"Tiger Woods will have a tremendous impact on the world of sports and will change the way people view the game of golf. He is one of a handful of special athletes who transcend their sports, the way Jordan has done in basketball, and McEnroe did in tennis.

—Nike press release, August 1996

MICHAEL JORDAN:

"I have so much admiration for this kid. He is one of my idols. I am in awe of what he's done. He certainly has the tools and work ethic to truly innovate the game."

—Associated Press

"I shot in the 70s when I was eight. I shot in the 60s when I was 12. I won the U.S. Junior Amateur when I was 14. I played in the Nissan Los Angeles Open when I was 16. I won the U.S. Amateur when I was 18. I played in the Masters when I was 19. I am the only man to win three consecutive U.S. Amateur titles. There are still golf courses in the U.S. that I cannot play because of the color of my skin. I'm told I'm not ready for you. Are you ready for me?"

At La Costa Country Club, at a 569-par-5 called The Monster, where nobody had ever reached the green in two, Tiger first cracked the ball past the spot where the tour's previous longest hitter, John Daly, had hit. From there, he could have just hit a couple of short shots and played it safe. But instead he pulled out a wood and risked it all—and made it.

JOURNALIST CHARLES P. PIERCE ON TIGER'S COMPETITIVENESS:

"It was a savage and wonderful choice that he made, the choice of a man who competes and who knows the difference between those days when you want to win and those days when you want to beat people, and who glories in both kinds of days. The choice he made to hit the wood was a choice he made not only for that day but also for a hundred others, when other golfers will be playing him close, and they will remember what he did, and maybe, just maybe, they will jerk it over the coots and into the pond. If that is the hand of God, it is closed then into a fist."

—GQ

"Nothing Woods has done would compare to winning a green jacket. His African-American heritage would make a victory in the tournament, in which no black was invited to play until 1975 and where every caddie was black until '83…a transcendent accomplishment. From a purely golf perspective, Woods would graduate from being the game's most talented player to its best, until further notice. And by winning a Grand Slam event at a younger age than Jack Nicklaus, Woods would be off to a flying start in his race against the record of the golfer with whom he is unavoidably compared."

—Sports Illustrated

EARL WOODS:

"This week Tiger will go into his major mode. That means he'll go to his house in Orlando, give himself a lot of solitude, do a lot of thinking and then work hard on what he decided he needs. When he calls me, we'll talk. And when he gets to Augusta on Monday, he will be ready and focused on winning."

—Sports Illustrated's GolfPlus *via the Internet*

TIGER BEFORE THE MASTERS:

"The week of a major, you have to eat, drink, think, dream—just everything—golf. That's what Faldo does. I'm sure that's what Nicklaus did. Obviously, I lack some experience. But being young and having a lot of energy and being psyched to play can also work to my advantage. I can get into that totally obsessed state maybe more easily than an older player, who has done it for years and has more going on in his life. The danger for me is overdoing it, trying too hard and losing patience. But I know how to focus. I've done it before."

—Sports Illustrated's GolfPlus *via the Internet*

JOURNALIST JAIME DIAZ:

"Augusta is made for Woods....More than any other course. Augusta National rewards 'talent shots,' the kind only a minority of the players blessed with power and excellent technique can pull off, and Woods has more talent than anyone else."

—Sports Illustrated

MIKE (FLUFF) COWAN, TIGER'S CADDIE:

"Expectations are never good for a golfer. But if Tiger can play well—not necessarily super—he's going to take that place apart."

—Sports Illustrated's GolfPlus

"Basically, what Jack did was play to the safe side on the par 3s and par 4s make a bunch of tap-in pars, then kill the par 5s. That's the way I want to play. It's such a deceptive course. It looks wide open, but it's really got a pretty narrow route if you want to get a good angle at the pin. That's what Faldo is so good at. And if you want to get your irons close, you usually have to lean them away from the pins and on these tiny spots. Naturally, I learned all this the hard way."

—Sports Illustrated's GolfPlus

Journalist Larry Dorman:

"The hip hype that has accompanied Woods's move into the professional ranks is both understandable and regrettable."

—New York Times, *September 1, 1996*

Curtis Strange:

"He's strong in every department. We've been talking about a player like this for a long time, and now he's here. Tiger has that competitive meanness. When he's on the course, he will tear your head off and spit down your neck. That might sound harsh, but you've got to have that if you're going to be great."

—*Titleist press release, April 1997*

TOM WATSON:

"The key is to continue and not let up. How long can you do that? I was able to do it for about seven years. Jack Nicklaus did it longer than anybody. No question the money is corrupting. The more money you make, the less you try. Tiger says he wants to win every tournament. That is a unique attitude. It comes down to heart."

—Titleist press release, April 1997

NICK FALDO ON TIGER:

"I've got to do some extra sit-ups."

—Sports Illustrated's On-Line Golf

MARK CALCAVECCHIA:

"Us cagey veterans, we're going to want to kick this kid's butt."

MARK O'MEARA, TIGER'S NEIGHBOR IN ORLANDO:

"Last week, the fans were really behind me. They were saying, 'You're the best' and things like that. But there were some on Saturday who said things like 'Next time Tiger's gonna clip you.'

"I love competition. I love feeling that little bit of tingling going on inside. When you have a guy like Tiger Woods coming on and the yelling, it's the best."

—Sporting News, *February 11, 1997*

COLUMNIST JOE BURRIS:

"He hit the dimpled white sphere off the tee so high, so far, that for a moment it got lost in the misty, bright blue sky. Then the ball sailed downward, took two bounces to the right of the cup, and skirted underground like a field mouse running from a predator."

—Boston Globe, *September 2, 1996*

PAYNE STEWART AFTER TIGER'S WIN AT THE WALT DISNEY OLDSMOBILE CLASSIC:

"Tiger is the greatest thing that's happened to the Tour in a long time. He has brought incredible attention to golf at a time of year when football and the World Series always take precedence. Everything I've heard about him seems to be true."

—Associated Press, August 1996

TOM LEHMAN:

"I think Tiger's performance has got everyone feeling they have to improve or get left behind."

—Titleist press release, April 1997

"I really don't know how they see me. I look up to these guys, these are the guys I watched on TV growing up. But I go to every tournament trying to win. Otherwise you shouldn't even show up."

—Atlanta Inquirer

NIKE CEO PHIL KNIGHT, AFTER SIGNING TIGER TO AN UNPRECEDENTED $40 MILLION CONTRACT:

"People often tell me that Michael Jordan was the first superstar of the wired world. Well, today's world is a lot more wired. There are so many more ways for Tiger to touch people than there were for Michael that he could easily be as widely known around the world as any athlete today—and in a fraction of the time."

—Nike press release

HUGHES NORTON, IMG, WOOD'S MANAGEMENT COMPANY:

"Anyone with a brain in their head realizes that Tiger's deals benefit everybody. Not quite like in team sports, but everybody will get at least a nudge."

—Fortune, May 1997

NIKE CEO Phil Knight:

"You could see Tiger coming. I'd been following him since he was a kid. You could see he was not only going to be a great golfer, but that he had the total package. You could see he was going to be special."

—Nike press release

III. CHAMPION TIGER

A television audience of more than 44 million people in the U.S. alone, as well as hundreds of millions worldwide, saw Tiger Woods win golf's most prestigious event—the Masters in Augusta, Georgia. Not only did he win, but he broke every meaningful course record, and crushed his nearest competitor by winning by a record margin of 12 strokes.

The hype was finally fulfilled.

Journalist Michael Bamberger:

"Last Saturday night, in the long Augusta twilight, there was one man on the practice tee and one man in the tournament. He was Tiger Woods, and he had a nine-shot lead with one round remaining. The other 45 players in the field were playing in a different event, for a different prize. The inevitable was still a day away."

—Sports Illustrated

"Winning here will do a lot for that game of golf. I'm in a unique position because a lot of kids look up to me as a role model."

—*United Press International, April 13, 1997*

CHARLES BARKLEY:

"This is huge. It's like Arthur Ashe winning Wimbledon. It's a great day for me, and I hope all black people are as proud as I am."

—Los Angeles Times, *April 15, 1997*

BRYANT GUMBEL:

"The way he played and conducted himself was absolutely exceptional. All you can do is stand up and cheer. It is another crack in the armor of those people who want to say African-Americans are incapable of doing this or that. I'm applauding loudly."

—Los Angeles Times, *April 15, 1997* ·

"I wasn't the pioneer. Charlie Sifford, Lee Elder, Ted Rhodes, those are the guys who paved the way. Coming up 18 I said a little prayer of thanks to those guys. Those guys are the ones who did it."

—Sports Illustrated, *April 21, 1997*

Lee Elder was the first black to compete in the Masters in 1975. Lee drove from his Ft. Lauderdale home to Augusta to watch Tiger win, picking up a speeding ticket because he was so eager to see him win.

"I'm so proud. We have a black champion. That's going to have major significance. It will open the door for more blacks to become members here. It will get more minority kids involved in golf."

—Sports Illustrated, *April 28, 1997*

"I was thinking, 'Boy, I have a tough putt.' That was my thought…my focus never left me, is what I'm trying to say. Even with all the ovation I got, and everybody cheering me on—it was a special moment—I knew I still had business to do."

—New York Newsday, *April 21, 1997*

EARL WOODS:

"Winning the Masters is a rite of passage to elite status on the PGA Tour. Winning quiets certain critics and skeptics who said he hasn't done this or he hasn't done that."

—Los Angeles Times, *April 16, 1997*

NIKE CEO PHIL KNIGHT:

"You run out of superlatives. He's off the charts. We expected great things, but he's gone way beyond. He creates a lot of drama, even when he's way ahead."

—*CNN television interview*

"He told me he was proud of the way I played. He watched the entire tournament because he had the bad knee.

"It means a lot, you know. It's something I always dreamed of. Something any kid has dreamed of, to win the Masters, and I did it."

—Newsday

Jack Nicholson, taking time off from watching the Lakers:

"Tiger just about ended the sport on Saturday. Even to try some of the shots he does is amazing. Stars do a lot for the entertainment business."

—Sports Illustrated, *April 21, 1997*

Charlie Sifford, pioneer black golfer:

"He is playing that golf course like a man 40 years old. He is managing it like Jack Nicklaus."

—USA Today, *April 14, 1997*

Tom Kite:

"This seems to be the next generation. He has leap-frogged the rest of the field. It's a very historic moment."

—USA Today, *April 14, 1997*

"Augusta National was designed by Alister Mackenzie in 1931 and built for Bobby Jones, who was the greatest golfer of his time, winning 13 of 21 major championships he entered from 1921 to 1930. Jones wanted a course that had no rough and ample fairways so that the recreational golfer could enjoy it as much as the professional."

—USA Today, *April 14, 1997*

GOLF LEGEND JACK NICKLAUS, REFERRING TO THE COFOUNDER OF THE MASTERS:

"It's a shame Bob Jones isn't here. He could have saved the words for me in '63 for this young man because he's certainly playing a game we're not familiar with. If he's playing well, the golf course becomes nothing."

—Associated Press, *April 14, 1997*

"Coming off finals isn't easy, and because of that I couldn't practice. I was pulling all-nighters getting ready for finals. So, of course, I'm going to be at a disadvantage."

—*Stanford University press release, April 14, 1996*

EIGHTY-THREE-YEAR-OLD GOLF LEGEND CHARLES YATES:

"I've seen every Masters and played in the first 11. I thought I'd seen everything, but Tiger Woods gives a new dimension to this tournament."

—USA Today, *April 14, 1997*

TOM KITE, WHO FINISHED A DISTANT SECOND IN THE 1997 MASTERS, A RECORD 12 STROKES BEHIND TIGER:

"I don't know how you rate this. Certainly to go 18-under par on this golf course is an incredible feat.

—Golf.com, *the Internet page of USGA*

TOM WATSON AT THE MASTERS:

"He's a boy among men, and he's showing the men how to play."

—USA Today, *April 14, 1997*

RICK SMITH, TEACHING PRO WHO WORKS WITH PGA TOUR PLAYERS:

"This golf course plays to every strength he has. He has distance and accuracy. He has a deft putting touch. And he has a great desire to play. Nicklaus had the same characteristics.

"The biggest thing that happened Saturday was the rain. That set the course up perfectly for him. It played right into his hand.

"For the next 10 years, Tiger needs to stop at all red lights and yield at all intersections."

—USA Today, *April 14, 1997*

"I knew I had to get through Amen Corner at even par. I knew I couldn't let up because all you have to do is put a few balls in the water on those holes and you're in trouble. I knew at the 16th hole that it was pretty much over. I knew I could bogey in and still win.

"You always dream. But you never dream of having such a big lead and winning like this. You dream of winning in a battle with someone.

"I had two things I wanted to do. I didn't want to make bogey. Twice people have shown 63 around here, so I thought if I didn't make a bogey I could win. If I shot 18 pars, I might have been in a play-off.

"To keep from making bogeys I knew I had to be patient. I thought my best chance to make birdies were on the par 5s."

—USA Today, *April 15, 1997*

JACK NICKLAUS:

"Tiger is out there playing another game. He's playing a golf course that he's going to own for a long time. He's going to win here a lot. I don't think I'd want to go back out and be 21 and compete against him. It's not my time anymore.

"It's his."

—United Press International, April 14, 1997

JAY LENO:

"How about Tiger Woods? You see how far he hit that ball? The only way he could have hit that ball further is if one of the Cubs pitchers were throwing it to him."

—From his monologue, April 13, 1997

RICK REILLY, EDITOR:

"So golf is all new now. Everything is a fight for place. Win seems to be spoken for. A babe in swaddling pleats with a Slinky for a spine and a computer for a mind had just won a major by more shots than anybody this century. How does he top this? The Grand Slam?"

—Sports Illustrated, *April 21, 1997*

MIKE (FLUFF) COWAN, TIGER'S CADDIE:

"He may be 21, but he ain't no 21 inside those ropes."

—Sports Illustrated, *April 21, 1997*

BEN CRENSHAW:

"Something's changing. Something's about to pass."

—Sports Illustrated, *April 21, 1997*

The black caddies at the Masters were touched in a way perhaps nobody else was.

A CADDIE KNOWN ONLY AS "JAP":

"Am I excited? If golf was all black and one white guy was doing this, wouldn't you be? Hell, yes, I'm excited."

—Sports Illustrated, *April 21, 1997*

BARRY BARNES, CADDIE SINCE 1971:

"Tomorrow will be special. I'll be home to watch Tiger get the green coat. Everyone you see out here tonight, they'll be inside watching Tiger tomorrow. It's the same way everyone used to go inside and listen to Joe Louis on the radio."

—Sports Illustrated, *April 21, 1997*

Derrick Dent, caddie at Augusta:

"The *Augusta Chronicle* ran a column last week saying it was ludicrous for Nike to say that Tiger can't play some courses because of the color of his skin. Well, let me tell you, there's a course in Augusta called Green Meadows—maybe Tiger Woods can play it, but Derrick Dent can't. And it is because of the color of my skin. There's no actual rule, it's just unwritten: You don't go there."

—Sports Illustrated, *April 21, 1997*

Michael Jordan after the Masters:

"He is going to endure certain things and he's got to deal with it. He has to be Tiger Woods. He can't be Michael Jordan, he can't be Dr. J, he can't be Charles Barkley.

"He's a great guy. If I can be any help to him, I'll give him any advice that he asks for. My responsibility to Tiger Woods right now is to be a friend.

"What he's going to be remembered for is what he does on the course. We all know what he's capable of. We've seen it."

—Associated Press, April 22, 1997

Masters founder, the late Clifford Roberts:

"As long as I'm alive, golfers will be white, and caddies will be black."

—Sports Illustrated, April 21, 1997

TIGER, PUTTING ON THE TRADITIONAL GREEN JACKET FOR THE
WINNER OF THE MASTERS:

"Green and black go well together, don't they?"

—Sports Illustrated, *April 21, 1997*

JACK NICKLAUS:

"Arnold Palmer and I both agree that you could take his Masters and my Masters and add them together, and this kid should win more than that. This kid is the most fundamentally sound golfer I've ever seen at almost any age."

—United Press International, April 13, 1997

TOM WATSON:

"He's got the heart of a lion. He has what it takes to dominate a field. He has proven he is a winner. He may be the type of player who comes along once a millennium."

—Golf.com, the Internet page of USGA

"Last year, Phil Mickelson won four tournaments. If you win the right four, that's the Grand Slam. Your game has to peak at the right time, and you have to be lucky."

—*Associated Press, April 22, 1997*

IV. THE RACE CARD

As much as we all would like to be able to pretend that all the attention that has been heaped on Tiger has been because of his extraordinary talent and accomplishments, the sad fact remains that there is a factor that has been there all along, both holding him back and pushing him forward. Tiger's mixed racial heritage combined with his excellence in golf, a sport whose traditions are steeped in prejudice and exclusion, has made the story of his triumph one that transcends mere athletic achievement.

Or, put more simply: a man wins the Masters every year. A black man won the Masters for the first time ever in 1997.

But along about the time everyone is slapping themselves on the back, congratulating one another on what an advanced society we now have, in which racial differences no longer matter, a couple of reminders crop up to remind us all how far apart we still really are.

LEE ELDER, THE FIRST BLACK GOLFER AT THE MASTERS:

"You'd walk through the crowds and hear, 'He shouldn't be here.' It made me feel wonderful watching him win. We needed it to get rid of all those ghosts hanging in those trees."

—USA Today, *April 14, 1997*

Woods says that his racial background is best described by the word CABLINASIAN. He is one-fourth black, one-fourth Thai, one fourth Chinese, one-eighth white, and one-eighth American Indian. Woods says that it bothers him when people call him an African-American.

"It does. Growing up, I came up with this name: I'm a Cablinasian.'

Woods checked off Asian and African-American on official forms.

"Those are the two I was raised under and the only two I know. I'm just who I am. Whoever you see in front of you."

—Los Angeles Times, *April 27, 1997*

Fuzzy Zoeller after finishing his round at the Masters:

"That little boy is driving well and he's putting well. He's doing everything it takes to win. So you know what you guys do when he gets in here? You pat him on the back and say congratulations and enjoy it and tell him not to serve fried chicken next year. Got it? Or collard greens or whatever the hell they serve."

—CNN

Fuzzy Zoeller a day later:

"My comments were not intended to be racially derogatory, and I apologize for the fact that they were misconstrued in that fashion. I've been on the Tour for 23 years and anybody who knows me knows that I am a jokester. It's too bad that something I said in jest was turned into something it's not, but I didn't mean anything by it and I'm sorry if I offended anybody. If Tiger is offended by it, I apologize to him, too.

"I was merely making reference to the Champions Dinner. In fact, when I hosted the dinner I served fast-food hamburgers. I have nothing but the utmost respect for Tiger as a person and an athlete."

—Associated Press, April 21, 1997

Tom Lehman a day later:

"I know Fuzzy and it was obvious to me that he was attempting to be funny. He probably would have said the same thing to Tiger's face and they both would have yukked it up.

"It wasn't the best timing and it wasn't in good taste. I'm sure he was making an attempt at a joke and it didn't come out right. But it's not appropriate."

—*Associated Press, April 21, 1997*

FRED COUPLES ALSO RUSHED TO FUZZY'S DEFENSE:

"Off-the-wall comments are made all the time. There was nothing racist about it. We don't have any problems like that out here. I don't think it's a big deal, and I'm sure Tiger doesn't. But I'm sure there are a lot of people around the world that do. And I'm sure Fuzzy wishes he wouldn't have said that."

—*Associated Press, April 21, 1997*

COMEDY CENTRAL:

"With Tiger Woods's victory at the Masters, there remain only two sports left still dominated by white athletes...hockey and church-burning."

—via the Internet, April 28, 1997

TIGER'S COUSIN VACHIRA POONSWAT, AFTER SEEING HIM PLAY IN A TOURNAMENT IN THAILAND:

"Tiger has some American characteristics, but his behavior is more Thai. He is shy, and the people see his smile, his smiling eyes, and the peace he carried with him, and he is like them. Yes, he is darker, but there is no color in Thailand. We judge each person by his behavior.

—Time magazine's international edition, February 17, 1997

TIGER ON RACISM IN THAILAND:

"I don't get the hard looks here that I sometimes get in the States. The Thai people are kind, and I feel more accepted."

—Time *magazine's international edition, February 17, 1997*

COLUMNIST SANDY GRADY, ON THE COMPARISONS BETWEEN TIGER AND JACKIE ROBINSON, THE MAN WHO BROKE THE COLOR BARRIER IN BASEBALL:

"Since that moment when he walked up the Masters' final fairway, hugged his father and turned a glorious 1,000-watt grin on America, we've been swooning in Tigermania—the gaudy adulation we once gave generals who won wars or astronauts who made a pit stop on the moon.

"But it's harder to cut through the media blare, to separate hype from reality and wonder: What, beyond the *GQ* covers and TV puffery and Nike ads, will Woods mean to the country? Beyond his lynx-like swing, who is Tiger? Well, first, not to sound too harsh about it, he's not Jackie Robinson."

—USA Today

"Because Woods's Masters triumph came two days before the 50th anniversary of Robinson's breaking the baseball color line, Tiger and Jackie seemed intermingled in the hullabaloo. But there's no comparison.

"America was a different place in 1947. Robinson reined in his anger despite beanballs, N-words, and death threats Woods hasn't endured. No bench jockey in the Masters crowd held up shoes and taunted, 'Here boy, gimme a shine.' Tiger grew up in an Orange County, California, suburb, played at country clubs, hit balls on *The Mike Douglas Show* when he was three, and went to Stanford. Robinson's rough life made him a political activist. Doors swung open for Tiger; he didn't have to knock them down."

—USA Today

Baseball legend Hank Aaron:

"Woods is a young person who demonstrates to the dark world that you can play sports and be a success, but get an education."

—*Associated Press Online, April 21, 1997*

Norman Baker, Sports History professor at State University of New York:

"[Golf is] still viewed as a sports of the upper economic echelon. The closest to an outsider breaking in has been Lee Trevino. Tiger Woods is the first black player to have the promise of that level of performance. No non-white players have had his superstar potential."

—Atlanta Inquirer

"…golf historically has been a wealthy white man's game. For years, private country clubs erected de facto discriminatory policies—if not explicit bylaws—that kept women, Jews, blacks, and others off the course. Many of those barriers began to crumble…[but] even so, all-white clubs remain. Although minority golfers can play on more courses now, they haven't always received the warmest welcome.

"Even Woods received death threats when he played in the Los Angeles Open in 1992, according to his father. And at the Byron Nelson Classic in Irving, Texas, two years ago, two women armed with pistols were arrested on the course where Woods was practicing.

"…barriers like these at private clubs have contributed to a glass ceiling in the workplace for some women and minorities.…Golf is more than just a sport. It also can act as entree into the top rungs of power and influence, as political, business, and community leaders network and talk up deals."

—Atlanta Inquirer *via the Internet*

ANONYMOUS CORPORATE SPONSOR, REVEALING THAT NOT EVERYONE IN GOLF IS HAPPY AT THE SUCCESS OF A NON-WHITE:

"There are clearly some people in the golf community who are ambivalent about Tiger Woods. He's altering people's perception about what golf means. He's a guy who's African-American, not the white, middle-class kid who grew up in the country club.

"A lot of people in golf were happy with that image, that elitism.

"It's what they sold. Now, right before their eyes, he's redefining what the sport of golf is, and they're not happy about it."

—Fortune, *May 12, 1997*

TOMMY FULCHER, 14, SON OF A BLACK COMMUNITY ACTIVIST IN SAN JOSE:

"Because Tiger is black, it shows me I can do this, that maybe I can accomplish what he does. It also makes me say to myself, 'Why can't there be more like him?' "

—San Jose Mercury News

EARL WOODS:

"Tiger's a human being. Where he comes from is really academic. He's not one race, and to say he is, is a lie that would be denying his mother's existence. Sure, if you ask him, he'll say he's black, then seconds later say, 'Yes, I'm Asian,' and be proud of both. All the black community has to do is watch his actions. All it has to do is watch the kids in the black communities when Tiger's with them. Kids can spot a phony in a heartbeat, and there is nothing in his face that says, 'I'm better than you.' It's rather 'I'm one of you.'"

—Associated Press, April 21, 1997

ROY S. JOHNSON, SPORTS EDITOR:

"...golf was once lily-in-a-snowstorm white....It was widely viewed as a game for wimpy, rich-kid punks from the suburbs who lacked any discernible athletic skill. I once hid my own burgeoning interest in golf from my black friends rather than risk being chided for playing a 'white man's game,' as most of them have called it.

"I no longer have to hide my passion for the game from other blacks. Coinciding with the growth of the black middle class, many African-Americans have embraced a game they once despised for its racist past. Now almost all of my black friends play golf, and it's rare when I meet a black professional who doesn't. Many even belong to private clubs, the bastions of whiteness that once symbolized golf's exclusionary tone."

—Business Week

DAVID FALKNER, AUTHOR OF A BOOK ON JACKIE ROBINSON:

"What Tiger has done is less significant than what Jackie Robinson did. Robinson was a person up against a national color barrier rather than a color barrier in one section of society. Jackie...helped to trigger the civil-rights movement. As spectacular as Tiger Woods's accomplishments are, I don't think they have the same social significance."

ALAN PAGE, PRO FOOTBALL HALL OF FAMER, AND AN ASSOCIATE JUSTICE OF MINNESOTA SUPREME COURT:

"We as a society like to look at the short term for long-term answers. This is a very young man who has a lot to contribute and will face a lot of challenges along the way. That's what life is about. Hopefully, he will grow and mature in ways that make what we see today even better."

—Associated Press, April 16, 1997

"Race might be an overblown [issue] in such fully integrated sports as basketball or baseball. But golf is still difficult to penetrate. Some of the clubs are still closed. So I guess that is why a lot of minorities don't play the game. So if you classify me as African-American or Asian-American, that's O.K. for now because golf has been predominantly a Caucasian sport. I think as more minorities enter the game and the influx of golfers increases...that issue is sure to become a dead issue.

"From my view, I don't think I've transcended the issue of race, but I might have. It's just kind of hard to see from my side sometimes.

"I've been kicked off courses just for the color of my skin. I've had hate mail, death threats, the whole nine yards. It's positive because it shows people are now being influenced by how I play. It's part of life, it's part of being in a sport which is predominantly Caucasian. Society is changing into this new era and, unfortunately, it's going to take some time."

—*Reuters*

Columnist E. R. Shipp:

"The public fury that followed Zoeller's remarks about Woods was wildly disproportionate to the offense. But such is that state of race relations in the U.S. that many blacks easily assumed the worst about Zoeller. And a news media stung by issues of race then turned Zoeller's lame attempts at humor into what it never was: yet another example of racism in America.

"I look forward to a day when race is no longer the prism through which we view each other. Then the reaction to a Fuzzy Zoeller won't be a national debate, but a chuckle. Or, if the joke is bad, a groan."

—New York Daily News

BRYAN BURWELL, COLUMNIST:

"As Zoeller walked away, you could hear laughter off camera. Someone other than Zoeller thought this was funny.

"The enlightenment was supposed to have arrived by now. Fifty years seemed long enough of a wait. But a half century after Jackie Robinson isn't enough time in some circles. In some circles—maybe with just enough liquor to heighten this tasteless brand of lowbrow humor, or just the right friends snickering to make everything seem acceptable—nasty, ignorant jokes will still be told.

"And the laughter won't be too far removed from the true sentiments in this circle of friends."

—The Sporting News

"I respect Fuzzy as a golfer and as a person, and for the many good things he has done for others throughout his career. I know he feels badly about the remarks. We all make mistakes, and it is time to move on.

"I accept Fuzzy's apology and hope everyone can now put this behind us.

"At first, I was shocked to hear that Fuzzy Zoeller made these unfortunate remarks. His attempt at humor was out-of-bounds and I was disappointed by it.

"But having played golf with Fuzzy, I know he is a jokester; and I have concluded that no animosity toward me was intended."

—*United Press International, May 2, 1997*

IMG Spokeswoman Bev Norwood:

"We absolutely did not hang Fuzzy out to dry. Tiger wasn't going to say something he didn't mean, so he carefully considered his statement."

—Los Angeles Times, *May 2, 1997*

Columnist Tim Keown:

"Woods is no different from any other athlete. Put bluntly, it's not in the best interest of a megastar pro athlete to adopt causes and take public stands, whether it be against racism or war or cholesterol.

"We often fail to take into account the nature of the athlete's life. He was groomed, shaped, and stuck with being a golfer by his father, who claims his son will do more good for humankind than any human since Christ.

"Tiger Woods isn't going to change the world.

"But he might change golf.

"Let's leave it at that."

—San Francisco Chronicle, *April 17, 1997*

V. TIGER'S IMPACT AND HIS FUTURE

A hoary old golf adage has always read: "You can learn more about a man in 18 holes of golf than in 18 years of conversation."

This is how it works: A couple of businessmen are sizing each other up, mentally chewing over the idea of what it would be like to go into business together. They play a round of golf. One guy is cautious, but as regular as a metronome—not trying to hit the ball long, but not making any mistakes either. The other is all over the course, crushing huge drives one minute, then skulling a worm-burner a couple of yards the next. He's leaving nothing in the bag, trying daring, outrageous shots, and although he fails sometimes, sometimes he connects, too.

Wanna bet their attitudes toward business are anything like the way they play golf? One steady, taking no risks, following a plan of attack exactly, the other flying by the seat of the pants, going wherever inspiration takes him.

Well, here's the thing about Tiger: he's both guys. Impossible shots—through trees, over water, curving in midair to miss a blimp—nothing but cup. He takes risks, but his skill, his training, his unshakable mental focus, all make what seems to be a wild toss of the dice as sure a thing as betting on the sun to rise.

And the best thing is, he's just gotten started.

"If I continue on the path of where I want to go, it is only going to get worse. I don't want to go into seclusion or hide away from everything. Because that's not right, not fair to the public. You have to be very receptive to it. Accept it, and that is the way it has to be."

—Golf.com, the Internet page of USGA

COMEDY CENTRAL:

"Now that Tiger Woods's career has peaked, golf experts say he can look forward to 50 years of steady weight gain, alcoholism, and increasingly undignified endorsement deals."

—*via the Internet*

LEWIS JONES, DEPUTY MEDIA DIRECTOR AT J. WALTER THOMPSON:

"You don't know what young stars are going to say once the press gets to them. He looks like he can handle it, but I am not sure that he has had as much as he is going to get."

—*Business Week*

JOURNALIST CHARLES P. PIERCE, ON THE INFLATED TIGER MYTHOS:

"I do not believe the following sentence: 'I don't think he is a god but I do believe he was sent by one.' This sentence presumes, first, that there is a God and, second, that He busies himself in the manufacture of professional golfers for the purpose of redeeming the various sinful regions of the world.

"Earl Woods asks, 'Can't you see the signs? Tiger will do more than any other man in history to change the course of humanity.'

"I do not believe that Earl Woods knows God's mind. I do not believe that Earl Woods could find God's mind with a pack of bloodhounds and Thomas Aquinas leading the way. I do not believe that God's mind can be found on a golf course as though it were a flock of genuine American coots. I do not believe—right now, this day—that Tiger Woods will change humanity any more than Chuck Berry did."

—GQ

EARL WOODS ON THE GQ ARTICLE:

"That article created a deep hurt. In my opinion, he lost his swing because of it. It disillusioned him and stayed with him awhile because he realized that he had misjudged a situation. He thought, 'How could I have been so stupid?'

"It's going to be all right. Tiger hasn't lost his idealism or his enthusiasm. He's not turning from a positive into a negative person. That would be a complete rejection of his whole personality and purpose. Yes, he's got some scar tissue and he's gotten harder, but he needs to grow. As he says to me, 'Dad, I'm getting so damn tough.' He realized better than anyone that this is his life now and that he has to accept that which comes with it. No way has he lost sight of what he wants to accomplish."

—Sports Illustrated Online Plus, *April 1997*

"You have to protect your investments, and the good investment is the controlled image. We're not far from the day when top-flight athletes won't talk to newspapers or magazines or any other nonpaying outlet; they won't need to. Commercials and electronic sycophants (Jim Nantz springs to mind) provide the perfect, surprise-free format for the controlled image.

"Woods was the subject of a profile in *GQ*, and in it he tells some dirty (and shockingly bad) jokes. Within seconds of the story hitting the stands, the IMG demanded a retraction.

"It wasn't Woods demanding a retraction; it was the guys in suits on the 52nd floor."

—San Francisco Chronicle, *April 17, 1997*

BUTCH HARMON, TIGER'S SWING COACH:

"Earl is getting out of control."

—GQ

EARL WOODS:

"We had some dogfights, sure, because for a long time, Tiger just didn't know how to use me. But I told him, 'In the business world you're the boss, while I'm the assistant boss. I will give you total abject honesty and trust. You can't buy that from anyone else. In parent–child matters, I'm the dad and you're my son. There will be a different tone in my voice and in the language I use. You will know when I'm switching.'

"I'm in the middle of the eye of the hurricane. I can't appreciate the significance of it all because I can't see it. I'm too close. But soon, real soon, we'll see it all."

—Fortune, *May 12, 1997*

"This is my life, and anything that involves my time, I want to have a say-so. Other people are making decisions for me—if they think that's for me, then we're going to have a clash. And that's what you don't want.

"I'm still a kid. And I really think people forget that. I want my next spot to show me as still being a kid."

—Fortune, *May 12, 1997*

Tiger and Earl almost came to a parting of ways at the La Cantera Texas Open.

EARL WOODS:

"I walked into his room, and he was lying on his bed, face down. I just looked at him and said, 'Hey, I know how you feel.' Well, he jumped up and yelled, 'No, you don't know how I feel!' It was the first time in his entire life he had ever raised his voice to me. All I said was 'Tiger, I'm here for you, and if you don't know that, then you better start thinking.'

"I walked out of the room but came back a while later to tell him his tee time for the following day. When I walked in he looked at me and said, 'I apologize, Pop. I love you.' For a long time, we just stood there and hugged. I just wanted to be with him."

—Fortune, *May 12, 1997*

"This is the other half of the culture I was raised under. Thailand is my other home. It is my Mom's home."

KULTIDA, AFTER TIGER READ THAT SHE HAD SAID SHE WAS GOING TO DEMAND THAT HE MARRY A THAI GIRL:

"He said 'Mom did you say that? It's all over the world.' I never said that. The dadgum media got it wrong. All I said was that it would be nice if he did."

—Sports Illustrated's GolfPlus

Thais, impressed with Tiger's awe-inspiring drives, blasting far past the other players, impute supernatural assistance to explain how such might can come from such a skinny kid:

"Tiger is possessed with *palang chang*—elephant power."

—Time *magazine's international edition*

"Winning, period, is great—but to win here in Thailand is something special. It was a hard week with a lot going on, a lot of different forces on me, so I'm proud I overcame that, too."

—Associated Press, *February 1997*

NBA Commissioner David Stern:

"You have a charismatic star who redefines the way his sport is played, you've got a hunger for programming from an array of television networks, and you have a marketing colossus like Nike involved. It's a recipe for sports success and for the enormous growth of golf."

—Fortune, *May 12, 1997*

Sports agent Leigh Steinberg:

"Tiger has a chance to have an even broader appeal than Michael Jordan because we live in a time when communications is so instant and so universal that a guy sitting on an island in the Pacific could have watched him win the Masters live. Woods could have the most profound impact both inside and outside of sports of any athlete since Muhammad Ali."

—Business Week, *May 1997*

"I guess it all worked out, but these are situations I don't want to get into. All week I had no time to myself, no time to relax and have fun. I need to keep golf fun. I guess I had to learn the hard way."

—Sports Illustrated's GolfPlus

"Woods has, in fact, drawn a defining line of sorts for a sport that had long been lugging around the baggage of its past. Looking back, golf is narrow...the sport of really bad pants. Looking ahead, the view is broad and clear, and, well, cool. Jocks will play. Rock stars will play. Women will play. Rappers will play. Blacks will play. Most important, kids will play, which will alter the dynamics of sport in America, which is why that Sunday in Augusta meant so much more than a young man's first green jacket or a father's tearful hug."

—Fortune, *May 12, 1997*

JOE BEDITZ, PRESIDENT OF THE NATIONAL GOLF FOUNDATION:

"If Tiger could, say, attract a million new golfers to the game—people who otherwise would have never taken up the sport, or maybe taken it up later in life—the economic impact would be mind-boggling. That's quite a burden to put on a young man his age, but hey, Palmer wasn't much older than that when he emerged on the scene."

—Fortune, *May 12, 1997*

BRAD COOK, OWNER OF GOLF GALLERIA IN HONG KONG:

"There's been a terrific rise in retail sales after Tiger Woods. We've seen a major shift to younger golfers in Asia. The impact of Tiger on this crowd has been phenomenal."

—Business Week

**PAT FITZSIMMONS, OWNER OF GREEN EAGLE CO.,
A MINNEAPOLIS-BASED GOLF COMPANY:**

"Kids, kids, kids and their parents—that's what all of our distributors are telling me they're seeing all over the country. Our golf shops are saying that more kids are starting to come into the stores and trying out the equipment instead of waiting in the car."

—*Associated Press Online, April 28, 1997*

JIM MULLEN, JIM MULLEN'S HOTSHEET:

"He broke literary records, too. For the first time ever, the words *golf* and *excitement* were used in the same sentence."

—*via Internet On-line Humor*

"Success is coming at Tiger Woods with a rush that could topple a redwood. The President is on the horn. Corporate America is begging to give him millions to sell its wares. The golf business can suddenly divide its history into B.T. (before Tiger) and A.T. (after Tiger). And his father, Earl, among others, is talking of Tiger as a bridge between races, between nations—as a bridge to God knows where. General Powell in a Nike hat.

"All that being said, Tiger is not Houdini. Can he keep his eye on the golf ball? Build a bigger roster of Grade A endorsement deals? Satisfy the sure-to-increase demands of the PGA Tour, his handlers at IMG and TV? Stave off overexposure? Survive intense scrutiny? And serve as the role model that he thinks it is his duty to be?"

—Business Week, *April 28, 1997*

MARK O'MEARA:

"I know he's 21 and he's going to be absolutely great, but I'm not sure I would trade places with Tiger Woods."

—Associated Press, April 20, 1997

LON ROSEN, MAGIC JOHNSON'S AGENT AND PRESIDENT OF FIRST TEAM MARKETING:

"Coke, Gatorade, or Pepsi—you know that they are already making the calls. He's a natural for them. This kid is the real thing. . . . There are going to be people throwing all kinds of money at him. Five hundred grand here, a hundred grand there. But your public sees you for the kinds of things you endorse. You endorse second-rate products, and they start to think you're second-rate, too."

—IMG press release, April 1997

CORINNE PINSOF-KAPLAN, OWNER OF CHICAGO GOLF AND TENNIS CO.:

"There has been a tremendous impact, considering that it snowed in Chicago all last weekend. Woods is going to help my month significantly. People have been coming in for Titleist balls and Nike shoes. It's the best Nike has done in my store."

—Business Week

SEAN BRENNER, EDITOR OF TEAM MARKETING REPORT:

"It may be the end of loud plants and loud shirts. His taste in clothing might redefine what people wear on the golf course the way Michael Jordan's taste in basketball shorts influenced what basketball players wanted to wear on the courts."

—Business Week, *April 28, 1997*

"Quite frankly, I think it's an honor to be a role model to one person or maybe more than that. If you are ever given a chance to be a role model, I think you should always take it because you can influence a person's life in a positive light, and that's what I want to do. That's what it's all about."

—Business Week, *April 28, 1997*

LON ROSEN, MAGIC JOHNSON'S AGENT AND PRESIDENT OF FIRST TEAM MARKETING, ABOUT A SIT-DOWN BETWEEN MAGIC AND TIGER:

"Magic told him, 'There's going to be a lot of people who are pulling at you. You just have to be yourself—not who they want you to be."

—Business Week, *April 28, 1997*

MARK THOMAS, HEAD PRO OF KILLIAN GREENS:

"I've had a half-dozen people call me for lessons directly because of Tiger. They were watching the Masters and said, 'I think I'll give this a try.' "

—Miami Herald, *April 30, 1997*

STEFANIE JENSEN, 10-YEAR-OLD GOLFER:

"I'm relearning the stance, the form. I haven't been out for what, four or five weeks? Before Tiger Woods won the Masters.

"It seems pretty cool somebody younger can do pretty good as opposed to someone older. My favorite player is probably Tiger. It was Freddie Couples, but it's Tiger Woods now."

—San Jose Mercury News

BOB MEJIAS, HEAD PRO AT SANTA TERESA IN SAN JOSE:

"I've never seen so many young kids that are out here. We've got kids that are 9, 10, 11 years old, hanging out, hitting balls, asking questions. I don't have any question that it's in response to Tigermania.

"It's not a sport like football where it's 'Kill, kill, kill,' or baseball where you yell, 'Batter, batter, batter.' It was a matter of educating them."

—San Jose Mercury News

AUDREY LEUNG, 9, AFRAID HER MOM IS PUSHING HER:

"I told my mom, 'I'm afraid you want me to be a champion like him.' She said, 'No, I don't expect you to be a champion. I just want you to play and have fun.'"

—San Jose Mercury News

Marques Storga, 10:

"Tiger is one of my favorite players. He's the best golfer I've ever seen. I'm thinking of that one shot from between those three tall trees. I think that was a pretty good shot."

—San Jose Mercury News

Sheamus Mullen, manager at Range Land USA:

"Tiger Woods is bringing people out here, that's just the way it is. It's like *Happy Gilmore.* When that movie came out, kids came here swinging clubs like hockey sticks, like Happy Gilmore. Kids are seeing something they're not normally interested in and saying 'Hey, that's not that bad.' "

—San Jose Mercury News

JOURNALIST CANDACE MURPHY:

"Golf's popularity among kids may be as fleeting as youth. Golf is a game of etiquette, discipline, concentration, and serenity. They are traits not normally associated with an increasingly 'extreme' sports world."

—San Jose Mercury News

RICK BRADLEY, WILLIAM MORRIS AGENCY:

"He translates to the MTV generation a lot more than he does to the inner city."

—Business Week, *April 28, 1997*

TIGER WOODS ON HIS POTENTIAL:

"In order for the game to become hip and appealing to young people, they have to understand the history of the game. This history of the game is that it's always been an elitist type of sport in which only a person with a substantial economic base could play. And obviously, not all families have that.

"And I think that golf needs a person who is young enough and a lot like masses of kids to present this game to them as a sport that they, too, can play. And right now, I seem to be the one who is in that position. But a lot of other people are right behind me."

—Business Week, *April 28, 1997*

"The tough decisions get easier with experience. I'm only 21, I'm learning. I've had to learn from experience, and I'm learning a lot very quickly."

—Business Week, *April 28, 1997*